AMALIENBORG

Previously published:
ROSENBORG
English edition 1996

Pictured on the previous page: Chimney-piece and mirror in the Gala Room of Christian VII's Palace. Pictured on the facing page: François Boucher's overdoor for the Gala Room in Christian VII's Palace symbolizes one of the geniuses of art: architecture. The painting is situated above the door leading into the Gallery facing the garden.

Text
OLE NØRRING
GERDA PETRI
KJELD RASMUSSEN
CLAUS M. SMIDT

Editor of text and illustrations
KJELD RASMUSSEN

AMALIENBORG

THE ROYAL PALACES, CHAMBERS AND GARDENS
THE ROYAL DANISH COLLECTIONS

BORGEN

Amalienborg
© Borgens Forlag 1999
Published by:
Borgens Forlag,
Valbygaardsvej 33
DK-2500 Copenhagen, Valby
Typographic design: Anne Rohweder MDD
Repro and printing: Narayana Press
Translation into English: Dan A. Marmorstein

ISBN 87-21-00980-5

1st edition, 1st printing 2000

Published with support from:

Kong Christian Den Tiendes Fond
Margot og Thorvald Dreyers Fond

Photos and illustrations:
Front and back covers: Thomas Wilmann
Thomas Wilmann: 1, 2, 7, 11, 14, 15, 18, 22,
27, 30-43, 49-76, 78-87, 89-91, 93-94.
Ole Kristensen: 13, 19-21, 23-25, 97-100,
102-111.
Klaus Møller: 75.
Kjeld Rasmussen: 17, 28.
Kit Weiss: 101.
The Royal Library's Collection of Prints and
Drawings: 7, 8, 16.
Alex Christiansen, adapted by Anne Rohweder:
12 (ground-plan).
Palaces and Properties Agency, adapted by
Anne Rohweder: 112 (garden-plan).

Table of CONTENTS

6   HISTORY   *Amalienborg and the Frederiksstad*

26   **CHRISTIAN IX'S PALACE**   *Residence of Her Majesty*
Schack's Mansion   *Queen Margrethe II*

44   THE BIRTHDAY   *On the Palace Square, the Queen is given*
an ovation on the 16th of April

48   **FREDERIK VIII'S PALACE**   *Residence of Queen Ingrid*
Brockdorff's Mansion

58   **CHRISTIAN VII'S PALACE**   *Representation chambers*
Moltke's Mansion   *and guest apartments*

88   THE PALACE GARDENS   *The garden behind*
Christian VII's Palace

92   **CHRISTIAN VIII'S PALACE**   *Residence of Crown*
Levetzau's Mansion   *Prince Frederik and Royal Danish Collections*

106   THE AMALIEGARDEN   *The public palace park*
on the waterfront

HISTORY

Amalienborg and the Frederiksstad

CLAUS M. SMIDT

In a manner of speaking, Amalienborg made its entrance as a royal residence overnight. It was late in the night of February 26, 1794 that the magnificent Christiansborg Palace burned to the ground. Insufficient sweeping of the chimneys and a badly conceived system of flues along with an improvident lay-out of the interior and use of the palace were all contributing factors to the catastrophe. Each of the huge attics above the palace's four wings was being utilized to store surplus timber whereas intersecting fire walls had not yet been deemed necessary. For quite some time there had been a threatening rumble in the chimney system of the Rococo palace. But no one had really taken notice. On the afternoon of February 26, a fire broke out on the storey occupied by the Crown Prince and facing the Riding Grounds. Before the night was over, the pride of the realm was a totally gutted heap of rubble.

The tragedy left the Royal Family without a roof over their heads. At the time, the family consisted of the mentally disturbed King, Christian VII; his son, the Crown Prince (later to be Frederik VI) and Crown Princess Marie; the Queen Dowager Juliane Marie and her son, the Heir Presumptive, Frederik, and his Princess, Sophie Frederikke; and finally, the Crown Prince's sister, Princess Louise Augusta, and her Consort, Frederik Christian, Duke of Augustenborg. The King spent the first night with his son and daughter-in-law on Kongens Nytorv in the home of General H.W.v. Huth, situated in the old cannon foundry, the Gjethus, located on the very spot where Copenhagen's Royal Theater now stands.

In the course of just a few days, however, everything fell into place, and Amalienborg became the country's new royal residence. The King was installed in the mansion that still today bears the name Christian VII's Palace. The Crown Prince and Princess took up residence with their daughter in the mansion that much later would come to be known as Christian IX's Palace, at present the residential palace of our Queen, Her Majesty Margrethe II. The Heir Presumptive and his wife and their four children set up house in the mansion that still bears the name of their eldest son, Christian VIII. Only the Queen Dowager and the Duke and his Consort, Princess Louise Augusta, settled in homes outside Amalienborg. Juliane Marie came to reside in Gyldenløve's small palace, the present home of the Håndværkerforening (Craftsmen's Guild), and the Duke of Augustenborg acquired Dehn's palace.

It might seem surprising that only one of the mansions at Amalienborg belonged to the King at the time. This was Frederik VIII's Palace, at present the residence of Queen Ingrid. It was acquired in the middle of the 1760s to be converted into an infantry cadet academy – a school for officers. The other three mansions were all privately owned. Although they are the hub of the Frederikstad, an area laid out as far back as 1749 in order to commemorate the 300th anniversary of the royal line of Oldenborg on the Danish throne, all four mansions were erected at the expense of private citizens. The name Amalienborg can be attributed to Frederik III's Queen, Sophie Amalie. In 1670, the year before the King's death, she initiated the building of a castle on this very spot. The area south of what was then the newly established Citadel was special on account of its proximity to water. Thus, an intensive degree of pile-driving was called for in order to erect any kind of building on the site. Furthermore, drainage, with canals encircling the area, made it possible to lay out a park.

Sophie Amalienborg Castle did not stand for very long. In 1689, it was completely destroyed by fire. Later on, Christian V had grand plans that involved getting the Swedish architect, Nikodemus Tessin the Younger, to build a new residential castle on the former site of Sophie Amalienborg's edifice that was supposed to replace the old overbuilt Copenhagen Palace. These plans never materialized. But in the 1720s, a pavilion was erected on the approximate spot where the castle had once stood. At the same time, new customs buildings were constructed on Nordre Toldbod and after a while, timberyards were laid out to the east of the area between the harbour and the road leading to the customhouse.

Christian VIII's Palace, as seen from the roof of Christian VII's Palace.

It was not until 1749 that the park and the drill ground to the north became the center of a new project.

On the occasion of the impending 300-year anniversary of the coronation of Christian I, which had taken place on October 28, 1449, Frederik V resolved, in the autumn of 1749, to grant the area to Copenhagen's municipal authorities so that a new section of the city could be laid out for the benefit of the city's merchants. Details about the earliest schemes are unclear. However, at a meeting held at Jægerspris Castle on September 5, 1749, the King and his council definitively resolved to lay out the Frederikstad. The quarter's »birth certificate« is the royal ordinance of September 12 of the same year which proclaims that the monarch is donating the Amalienborg Gardens with the adjacent military parade grounds to »those of our subjects who, on the very same spot and ground, should desire to build«.

Since the institution of absolute monarchy in Denmark, the ever-changing kings had sought to set their special mark on the capital city. France, the leading nation among autocracies, served as a model. And it was the Sun King, Louis the XIV, who had set the example with the grandiose buildings in Paris and at Versailles. Especially conspicuous in this regard is the old Louvre, which was enlarged and modernized, as well as the newly erected palace at Versailles. In Paris in 1685, a private citizen had the Place des Victoires constructed in order to honour the King.

The architect for Place des Victoires was Jules Hardouin-Mansart, who was simultaneously building at Versailles. The concept is reminiscent of Amalienborg: a polygon (multi-faceted) square surrounded by uniform palaces, with a monument set up in the middle for honouring the monarch. A few years later, the same architect fashioned the Place Vendôme, also situated in Paris. It was especially during the reign of the Sun King's son, Louis the XV, that large-scale urban planning was successfully implemented. In a most direct way, this plan reflected the new societal order with the King in his place at the top of the pyramid in the societal hierarchy. Two royal squares created in France around the same time as the Frederikstad are the supreme examples of this design: Place de la Bourse in Bordeaux, with the sculptor J.B. Lemoyne's equestrian statue of Louis XV at its centre and the later Place de la Concorde in Paris, where Edme Bouchardon's equestrian statue depicting the same King was the crowning glory. In both places, the architect Ange-Jacques Gabriel was responsible for the plan and the architecture. In the Bordeaux project he worked in conjunction with his father, Jacques Gabriel.

Thus there was plenty of inspiration to fetch from France for Frederik V and his advisors. Here in Denmark, the attempts to create a new Copenhagen had so far been rather modest. Kongens Nytorv, with its various mansions built by peers of the realm, and Abraham César Lamoureux's equestrian statue of Christian V dating from 1689 was our first *place royale*. There was decidedly more grandeur to be found in Christian VI's extensive and complex Christiansborg Castle (erected in 1733-45) with its splendid Riding Grounds, its Marble Bridge and the opposite quarter situated alongside Frederiksholms Kanal. However, Copenhagen was still characterized by the medieval city's picturesque disorder and crooked streets.

The new Frederikstad, then, came to signify a crucial point of departure. From the beginning, the construction site, delimited by what is now Bredgade, Skt. Annæ Plads, Toldbodgade and the Esplanade, was almost rectangular and fell quite naturally around a north-south central axis, which would later be Amaliegade. Almost from the outset, the area also included the former Princess Charlotte Amalie's Garden, inasmuch as it was this site which was designated for the construction of the quarter's church. Actually, this site was situated to the west of the area. On the third day of the festivities celebrating the 300-year anniversary – October 30, 1749 – the Royal Family drove in a coach to this garden and Frederik V laid down the foundationstone for the Frederik's Church. The perpendicular axis was thereby determined and it was also alongside this axis (now Frederiksgade) that the King reserved the exclusive right to select the architects and the owners.

Apart from the church, »the square in the centre« (i.e., the palace square) was set aside for noblemen's palaces. For this task, royal master builder Nicolai Eigtved was called in to provide the plans. Although the equestrian statue of the monarch in the middle of the square was not actually included in the planning until 1750, when the versatile artist Carl Marcus Tuscher delivered the first sketch, the royal monument was undoubtedly an indispensable element of the Frederikstad from the very beginning. Contact with the man who was eventually to create the statue first came about in 1752, after the foreign minister J.H.E. Bernstorff had tried in vain to enlist the services of France's most famous sculptor, Edme Bouchardon. It was through the secretary of the legation in Paris, Joachim Wasserschlebe, that a younger artist was enticed to come to Denmark. Jacques-François-Joseph Saly, who was relatively unknown when he was called to Denmark – he had not yet tried out his skills with an equestrian statue – arrived in the country in the spring of 1753. Eventually, he came to be a most expensive acquaintance for the nation. In return, he gave his very best. Saly, with his depiction of Frederik V on horseback, created one of the most beautiful equestrian statues in the world, a work in total harmony with its surroundings.

Around 1750, Eigtved, the chosen architect, was the nation's most eminent royal master builder, held in favour by both the King and his powerful Lord High Chamberlain, Count Adam Gottlob Moltke. Nicolai Eigtved's life had taken on the dimensions of a fairy tale. The son of a crofter from the Haraldsted region, he had been trained as a gardener at the royal gardens. Later on, he went to Saxony and was educated further at the corps of engineers and he eventually became the court architect at the court of Christian

The French-born sculptor, Louis-Augustin le Clerc, made a drawing of Amalienborg, and J.M. Preisler engraved the motif in 1766, here with a project for the Frederik's Church, approved by the architect Nicolas-Henri Jardin but never realized. For a period of one hundred years, the church stood as Copenhagen's »Forum Romanum«.

Dessiné par Le Clerc.

Place Royale de Friderichstadt à Copenhague

Gravé par J. M. Preisler.

9

VI in 1735. The Saxon court employed several talented French architects, among them Jean de Bodt and Zacharias de Longuelune. It was their tempered approach to Rococo architecture that Eigtved picked up on. Before assuming his position in Copenhagen, Eigtved had seen with his own eyes the most modern examples of south-German and Italian architecture. In dignified competition with Lauritz de Thurah, Eigtved managed to become both Christian VI's and Frederik V's architect of choice.

Nevertheless, in the autumn of 1749, Eigtved had to compete with Thurah and Tuscher for the assignment of designing the four mansions at Amalienborg. Eigtved won the competition and the two rivals' projects are unknown today. The octagonal square and its buildings were formed entirely in accordance with Eigtved's drawings.

The four mansions were absolutely uniform in their exterior, with a predominant *corps de logis* (central building), conjoined with flanking corner pavilions by short one-storey gate wings (the wings did not have an additional storey added until later on, in 1794, when the Royal Family moved in). The sandstone-faced buildings are especially distinguished by their lively interchange between high and low, with their rusticated lower storeys and central sections in three bays with round-arched windows and door openings, and embellished with full columns in the *bel étage*. The mansions constitute Eigtved's entirely personal tender for »Danish Rococo«. However, there is no denying that the architect had allowed himself to be inspired by among other things the Japanisches Palais in Dresden and the Palazzo Madama in Turin. He knew both buildings well; he had seen them himself.

The prospective inhabitants of the Frederiksstad were given the lots free of charge. Furthermore, they were offered tax exemptions on the erected houses for a number of years. These were a few of the ways by which the construction in this part of the city moved forward. It was difficult enough to entice well-respected commoners to commit themselves to the task. Finding noblemen willing to buy the mansion sites proved even more difficult. All the buildings in the quarter called for expensive pile-driving, and the large houses especially needed extremely wealthy patrons. Presumably, King Frederik V almost had to coerce high-ranking courtiers to take on the roles of builders. However, one of them was an obvious candidate, Adam Gottlob Moltke, newly created Count of Bregentved, who built Moltke's Mansion, known today as Christian VII's Palace. Furthermore, Moltke retained Eigtved to design the interior of his home. His building became by far the most elegant of the four Amalienborg mansions. Moltke was a leading force behind the efforts for the entire project. Moreover, he was a member of the Ecclesiastical Building Commission and as chairman of the Asiatisk Kompagni he took the initiative in getting the company to provide the financing for the erection of the equestrian statue. Moltke acted with such firm resolve that when Eigtved died in the spring of 1754, the architect had already managed to complete the mansion. None of the other builders on the royal square were as resolute. One of them, the later Baron Severin Løvenskiold, had already been compelled in the same year to give up his mansion into the possession of Countess Anna Sophie Schack, because his estate was in bankruptcy. The Countess bought the still unfinished house in order to provide a residence for her grandchild, Count Hans Schack, upon the occasion of his wedding to A.G. Moltke's daughter, Ulrikke. This mansion is the present-day residence palace. After a fire in the latter part of 1754, young Schack built his mansion and moreover, he accomplished this while his castle in southern Jutland, Schackenborg, was being modernized in lush Jutlandian Rococo. It is this castle which is now in the possession of Prince Joachim and Princess Alexandra.

The last two palaces at Amalienborg were built by General Christian von Levetzau (later designated Christian VIII's Palace) and Privy Councillor Joachim von Brockdorff from the Nør Estate in Schleswig (later designated Frederik VIII's Palace). The latter died in 1763, and at that time, A.G. Moltke acquired Brockdorff's estate in South Jutland and as part of the bargain, Moltke also obtained the mansion at Amalienborg. A few years later, the mansion was sold to the King in order to become the Naval Cadet Academy.

The erection of the Frederik's Church, later to be known as the Marble Church, since it was built with the use of Norwegian marble, came to take a very long time. At first, it was obviously the intention that Eigtved was to take on the task. Prior to his death, he managed to propose four different projects for the church. At the suggestion of J.H.E. Bernstorff, Ange-Jacques Gabriel in Paris was consulted, and he too submitted a proposal. Lauritz de Thurah also came forward with a design. The final outcome, however, was that in 1755, Nicolas-Henri Jardin, a young French architect, was called in. Following the directives of his plans, the erection of a gigantic cupola church was set into motion in 1756. In the meantime, the stylistic idiom had changed from Rococo to a more classicist approach. The expensive enterprise made only slow progress.

*Queen Margrethe,
Prince Henrik and ship-owner
Mærsk Mc-Kinney Møller,
at the dedication of Saly's newly
restored equestrian statue.*

In 1771, Privy Cabinet Minister J.F. Struensee halted construction. After this, the half-completed church lay for more than a century as Copenhagen's veritable Forum Romanum. It was only through the aid of financier C.F. Tietgen that the completion of the Marble Church was accomplished in 1894. The church was completed in a Renaissance style according to sketches by the architect, F. Meldahl.

The summoning of N.-H. Jardin from France also entailed that in 1757, this architect redesigned several portions of the interior of Moltke's mansion. Among other changes, he created the beautiful dining hall in the *bel-étage* in the mansion's northern end as well as the graceful aviary in the palace garden.

1794 was the decisive year for Amalienborg. As a result of the catastrophic palace fire, the Royal Family purchased the three mansions which were not in royal possession and the Crown Prince asked the court architect, C.F. Harsdorff, to take chare of the interior design of both his own and his father's mansions. Most of the work was of a practical nature. The connecting wings, for example, had a second storey added in all the mansions, and the original semicircular vestibule in Christian VII's Palace was dismantled and an extra storey interposed. Harsdorff also used the opportunity to modernize some of the interiors. For this purpose, he made use of the services of his collaborator, the court decorator J.C. Lillie, who furnished the two mansions in English Adam-style. At the home of the Heir Pre-sumptive, in what later came to be Christian VIII's Palace, the painter N.A. Abildgaard was employed to decorate the palace with a distinctive taste that deviated perceptibly from Harsdorff's and Lillie's.

Something new at Amalienborg was the colonnade, which conjoined Christian VII's Palace with the later Christian IX's Palace. This construction also fulfilled a specific functional demand: the Crown Prince required a convenient connection to his father whenever he had to obtain the King's counter-signature on royal letters and resolutions.

Harsdorff accomplished this with something close to genius: there is hardly any dissonance between Eigtved's Rococo palaces and Harsdorff's Greek-inspired Classicism. Since it was expected in 1794 that the King and the Crown Prince would soon be moving back into the newly erected Christiansborg Castle, the colonnade was constructed solely in wood and painted the color of sandstone. No one ever expected that the arrangement at Amalienborg would become permanent. That was quite a miscalculation!

In order to bring the early story of Amalienborg to a conclusion, it remains to be told that in 1828, when Frederik VI betrothed his daughter Vilhelmine to Prince Frederik Carl Christian – the future Frederik VII, the King took over what had previously been the officer's school (the Infantry Cadet Academy), now known as Frederik VIII's Palace, and had the court architect J.H. Koch decorate the interior in late Empire style.

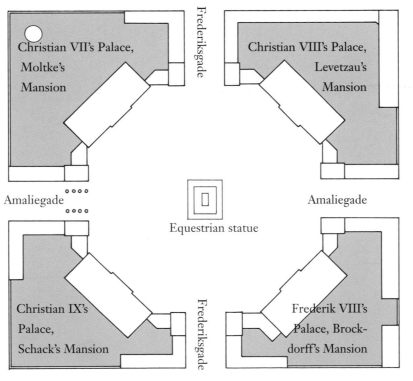

Christian VII's Palace, Moltke's Mansion

Frederiksgade

Christian VIII's Palace, Levetzau's Mansion

Amaliegade

Equestrian statue

Amaliegade

Christian IX's Palace, Schack's Mansion

Frederiksgade

Frederik VIII's Palace, Brockdorff's Mansion

Toldbodgade
The Amaliegarden

Seen from a bird's-eye perspective, Amalienborg's consummate geometry comes into view. At the bottom of the picture is Amaliehaven. Each of the palaces, however, also has its own green oasis, hidden away from the curious eye. Particularly the garden behind Christian VII's Palace, visible at the upper left, has retained its charm. The extensive roof running at right angles to Frederiksgade covers the Queen's Riding School, built in 1799-1800 by Boye Magens between the palace and the Bernstorff Mansion.

*On August 16, 1768, the equestrian statue of Frederik V was
mounted on its plinth. In the mansion on the left, Count A.G. Moltke
received the Royal Family as his guests for the special occasion.
Anonymous drawing in the Royal Library.*

With his equestrian statue, the
sculptor J.-F.-J. Sally has created a masterpiece.
The King is mounted majestically, like a Roman emperor,
on his handsome Frederiksborg horse.

C.F. Harsdorff built the Colonnade in 1794 after the Royal Family had taken up residence in Amalienborg when Christiansborg Castle was destroyed by fire. The structure was erected in wood and then painted the color of sandstone. No one ever imagined that it would remain standing for more than a few years! In the roofing, a concealed corridor connects Christian IX's Palace with Christian VII's Palace.

Frederik's Church – or as it is generally known: The Marble Church. The church was never completed according to the original plans. During the years from 1874-94, the financial magnate C.F. Tietgen saw to it that the church was finally finished. The architect F. Meldahl re-used Jardin's uncompleted walls and pillars, but transformed the church into a Renaissance building. The beautiful cupola is the sixth largest in all of Europe.

Preceding page: On the balustrades above Christian VII's Palace, these little boys or angel children are romping, enlivening the cornice. At the time the mansions were constructed, these figures were called kinder or putti [the plural form of putto, Latin for 'little boy'].

The frontispiece above Christian VII's Palace was originally embellished with the coat-of-arms of the building's owner, A.G. Moltke, and encircled, among other things, by the genius of fame. Today the cartouche is without motif and is terminated at the top with a royal crown.

Preceding page: On the balustrade at every corner of the
Amalienborg palaces, is a
vase with a fantasy mask.

The frontispiece above Christian VIII's Palace was first decorated with the
coat-of-arms of the building's first owner, General Levetzau. Presumably during the
reign of Christian VIII, who resided in this palace, the frontispiece was embellished
with the royal coat-of-arms. It is still encircled by allegorical Rococo figures.

On the cornice of Christian VII's Palace, the god Mercury, protector of trade and merchants, stands with his winged hat and a sack of coins in hand.

Standing as well on top of the same palace is the god Apollo, protector of the arts, with his bow in hand and quiver on his back. With these two god-figures the builder A.G. Moltke was being characterized both as an industrialist and a connoisseur of art.

The crowded cornice on top of
Christian VIII's Palace is embellished
with the presence of this goddess, whose
identity is hard to determine.

Notwithstanding the spear,
Minerva is the protector of art
and handicraft. She stands on
top of the same palace.

CHRISTIAN IX'S PALACE

Schack's Mansion

Residence of
Her Majesty Queen Margrethe II

OLE NØRRING

Every year on the Queen's birthday, as on the days of other great events in the Royal House, a »balcony scene« is enacted. The royal life guards parade in the palace square in their red gala uniforms. Thousands of children and adults waving the national flag, the Dannebrog, congregate on the square. At precisely 12:00 noon, the double doors of the Gala Hall are opened out to the balcony and the Queen and the Royal Family appear, cheered by thousands of spectators. We are all so very familiar with the scene! This is Christian IX's Palace, the present-day residence palace, and from the flag-bastion, the banner of Her Majesty Queen Margrethe II is floating in the breeze.

In the month of March 1750, Severin Leopoldus Løvenskiold, only thirty years old at the time, received a letter from the Lord High Chamberlain A.G. Moltke:

Most noble, esteemed and honourable Privy Councillor:

Having most graciously been so commanded I hereby would ascertain whether Your Honour might be disposed to erect one of the four large buildings at Amalienborg Square. I am assured that in such an event his Majesty would wish to further demonstrate His favours. I remain with utmost respect, Your Honour, Your obedient servant, A.G. Moltke.

The flattering offer was almost too much for a young man. Løvenskiold immediately replied in the affirmative, although he knew very well that he could not afford the cost. The young privy councillor received the King's donation deed for the site in May 1750. Actually, on the very same day he was to wed a general's nineteen-year old daughter, Charlotte Hedvig Numsen.

Young Løvenskiold started off by putting up a hoarding around his site, and the excavation commenced. Then came the bids from the artisans. They exceeded, by a long shot, the owner's financial capacities. Through the aid of loans and guarantees obtained from his father-in-law, General Numsen, construction was begun.

However, this mansion was not to be completed by Løvenskiold. When his economy was stressed to the breaking point, Løvenskiold succeeded in turning over the unfinished building to Countess Anne Sophie Schack, on April 23, 1754. At the time, Countess Schack was 73 years old and had been a widow for thirty-five years. Presumably, it was never her intention to move into the premises. Her idea was to assign the finished mansion to her grandchild, who was about to be married to the daughter of Lord High Chamberlain Count A.G. Moltke.

The process of construction met with difficulties. On the night of December 4, 1754, just as good progress was being made on the interior of the building – the walls and ceilings were already completed – a fire broke out, causing tremendous damages with ensuing major delays in the construction. The young noble couple, who were married on January 7, 1757, first moved into the mansion – now designated Schack's Mansion – in the spring and summer, even though certain records mention that they celebrated their honeymoon in the mansion. If so, it must have been in just a few rooms.

The mansion, however, was not yet fully the property of the young couple. It still belonged to the old Countess, Anne Sophie Schack. It was only after several economic transactions, with both Anne Sophie Schack and the young count's father-in-law, the Lord High Chamberlain, contributing large sums, that ownership of the mansion was finally transferred – at the end of 1759 – to Count Hans Schack. In 1760, however, Count Hans Schack was named Prefect of the County of Ribe and after this, the family seldom lived in the mansion at Amalienborg. In 1763, the young Countess Schack died in childbirth, at the tender age of 22. Soon afterwards, the Count remarried yet another countess from the Moltke family. She was the daughter of the Danish envoy in Germany.

By the year of 1768, we find Hans Schack's finances taking a turn for the worse. Eventually, Schack was compelled to request that his economy be put under administration. In 1773, the administrators decided to rent out the mansion. Hans Schack and

Every year, on their way to the New Year's reception at Christiansborg, the Royal Couple rides from Amalienborg in the golden state coach, accompanied by the Household Regiment's mounted escort.

The pillars on the face of
Christian IX's Palace
are thrown into relief by
the afternoon light of the sun.

his family then went to live permanently at Schackenborg, which today is the residence and property of Prince Joachim and Princess Alexandra.

Many well-known people, Danes as well as foreigners, lived as tenants in the mansion over the course of the next thirteen years, until the mansion changed hands in 1786, when Hans Schack transferred ownership of the property to his son, Count Otto Diderich Schack. He was the one who, in March 1794, after the fire at Christiansborg Castle, sold the mansion off as a residence for Crown Prince Frederik and his family for the sum of 26,590 rigsdaler. Indubitably, the extended period of renting out the premises, with the flux of so many different tenants, entailed considerable wear and tear on the mansion and consequently, a large-scale renovation project was set into motion shortly after the transfer of ownership.

For the first brief period, the Crown Prince and his family lived in his father's home, Christian VII's Palace. Subsequently the entire Royal Family took up temporary residence at Frederiksberg Castle while renovation in both palaces was being implemented. The definitive move into the two palaces took place in December. Of the Crown Prince and Princess's eight children, only two survived infancy, the Princesses Caroline and Vilhelmine.

In 1801, dark clouds loomed. In consequence of our close association with Napoleon, an English fleet under the command of Admiral Nelson was sent to Copenhagen, with the illustrious sea battle of Copenhagen on the second of April as a dramatic conclusion. On the following day, Admiral Nelson came ashore at Amalienborg to negotiate. Just a few days before, the Royal Family had taken up residence at Rosenborg. While Nelson awaited the arrival of the Crown Prince, he had dinner in the Crown Prince's palace, with the Crown Prince's aide-de-camp. The actual armistice was signed on the ninth of April.

In 1805, the Crown Prince travelled to Schleswig and further on to Kiel in order to assume command over the assembling of troops in Holstein under the third coalition with Napoleon. Soon afterwards, the rest of the family followed, and they took up residence in Kiel. The sojourn lasted for two years, and the palace at Amalienborg lay deserted all the while. It was not until the sixth and seventh of November, when the English bombardment of Copenhagen came to an end, that the Crown Prince returned and took up residence again at Amalienborg.

In 1808, King Christian VII died. The Crown Prince now became King Frederik VI and he kept his heir-to-the-throne residence as his residence palace up until his death in December 1839. Frederik VI's widow, Queen Marie, who was 72 years old at the time of her husband's death, stayed on in the palace and lived for another thirteen years.

After the death of Frederik VI, the palace was no longer the centre of everyday life at court. The new King, Christian VIII, had been living in what had been Levetzau's Mansion ever since 1794 when he had moved in with his parents as a seven-year old child. Later on, this palace came to be designated Christian VIII's Palace.

In 1863, the palace that had been Schack's Mansion once again became the King's residence. Upon the death of Frederik VII (who chose to reside in Christiansborg Castle) in 1863, it was resolved that the palace be transferred to the successor, King Christian IX's Civil List. And it was here, then, that King Christian IX and Queen Louise, who came to be known as »Europe's parents-in-law«, lived for the rest of their lives. The Queen died in 1898 and the King died on January 29, 1906. After the King's death, his son and successor King Frederik VIII and his five siblings resolved that their dear departed father's palace be officially designated Christian IX's Palace.

For as long as the children of Christian IX were still living, this palace continued to be their gathering point in Copenhagen. After the Russian revolution, the widow of the czar, the former Princess Dagmar, managed to escape from the Crimea, and by way of England, returned to Denmark. She then took up residence in Christian IX's Palace, with the express permission of Christian X. Eventually, she moved out to Hvidøre, where she ended her days.

Up until 1967, the palace was again uninhabited. It was then renovated as a residence for the Heiress Apparent, Princess Margrethe, and her Consort, Prince Henrik. Upon the death of Frederik IX in 1972, following tradition, it became the residence palace. Today, the palace is still inhabited by Her Majesty, Queen Margrethe II and His Royal Highness, Prince Henrik.

The disposition of the rooms inside the palace is somewhat reminiscent of Christian VII's Palace, but this palace is hardly as luxurious. The general stylistic features are Rococo and neo-Classicist. The central room, the Gala Hall, was designed by Harsdorff in 1794. Today, the palace attests to the fact that the Queen and the Prince, as a young couple, participated actively in the interior design while the palace was being restored and had their say about the choice of colours, etc. This palace now reflects the Queen's distinctive personal taste and her and the Prince's sharp eye for how their home was to be furnished. New art is beautifully blended with older art in this warm and intimate palace.

The band of the Royal Danish Life Guards
playing on Amalienborg Palace Square.

Chamber of banners.
When the Royal Couple is in residence at Amalienborg,
the Royal Life Guards' banners are kept in this room.

From the Gallery, the formal dining room of the Royal Couple,
there is access to the garden behind the palace. It is through this room
that one gains official admittance to the Queen's study.

Reception room.
Official visitors to Her Majesty the Queen
are received here by the aide-de-camp on duty.

The parade hall is the central room on the ground floor.
This room served as the vestibule of Schack's Mansion. In the vitrines,
the Prince has arranged his collection of glassware.

The Gala Hall, facing the palace
square. The door on the left leads
to the balcony.

The Royal Couple's private dining area. Behind the screens lies the butler's pantry,
connected by an elevator to the kitchen in the basement.
The tapestries were made during Queen Louise's day and feature Chinese motives.

The library is the smallest of the rooms in the bel étage.
What was once a stove recess has now become a showcase for
articles from the Queen's ethnographic collection.

The red saloon was originally the Queen's study.
The portrait of the young girl above the sofa is
painted by Jean-Baptiste Greuze.

The music room: The grand piano, a Steinway, is often played by the Prince.
The beautiful tapestry is a gift from the government and the Parliament.

*A corner of Prince
Henrik's study.*

The view from the balcony toward the Colonnade, Christian VII's Palace and Frederik's Church (the Marble Church).

The Royal Family on the balcony.

THE BIRTHDAY

On the Palace Square, the Queen is given an ovation every year on the 16th of April KJELD RASMUSSEN

The Royal House has played an essential role as a national focal point, especially after German troops occupied Denmark on the 9th of April, 1940, during the Second World War.

King Christian X took his daily morning ride through Copenhagen – alone, but well protected by the citizens who greeted him on his way.

Seven days after the beginning of the occupation, on the 16th of April 1940, Denmark's Crown Princess Ingrid gave birth to her and Crown Prince Frederik's first child, Princess Margrethe. The Princess was a »gleam of light in a dark time«.

Like her grandfather, King Christian X, little Princess Margrethe came to stand as a symbol and a ray of hope that some day Denmark would be free, once again.

Therefore, the people put out flags on that day, and ever since, Queen Margrethe's birthday, on the 16th of April, has been celebrated by thousands of children and adults cheering when the Queen – then, as well as now – appears on the balcony with her family at precisely twelve o'clock.

Be it sun, rain or wind, Denmark's family birthday on the Palace Square is always a festive affair.

His Royal Highness
Crown Prince Frederik,

Her Royal Highness
Princess Alexandra,

His Royal Highness
Prince Joachim,

Her Majesty Margrethe
II, Denmark's Queen,

His Royal Highness
Prince Henrik.

The Royal Life Guards' band has just arrived
at Amalienborg on its march through the city from
the barracks at Rosenborg Castle.

Facing Christian IX's Palace, residence of Her Majesty,
Queen Margrethe II, the Life Guards' band plays for their
Queen on the occasion of her birthday.

FREDERIK VIII'S PALACE

Brockdorff's Mansion

Residence of Queen Ingrid

OLE NØRRING

Among the four Amalienborg palaces, the one most easily identified by tourists is Frederik VIII's Palace. It is the only one with a clock on its façade. The clock was taken from Frederiksberg Castle and is said to have been mounted on the frontispiece so that the guard's watch in Christian VII's Palace – diametrically opposite – could keep an eye on the time to make sure that the changing of the palace guard would take place precisely.

The building's original patron was Baron Joachim Brockdorff, of the Nør family line, and thus from the duchies. He was born in 1695 and was a man of ripe age when he received his deed for the site from the King in 1750. Brockdorff did not live long enough to derive much enjoyment from the mansion, which was finished in 1760. Both he and his wife, born Christine Sophie Reventlow, passed away in 1763 and the mansion was acquired by the Lord High Chamberlain A.G. Moltke. In 1765, King Frederik V took over the palace, only one year before his own demise – in exchange for 52,000 rigsdaler. It thus became the first of the four Amalienborg palaces to be owned by a king. In 1767, the palace was converted into an infantry cadet academy – a school for officers. At that time, all the money belonging to the state belonged to the King and the King defrayed the expenses for the army and the navy.

The interior of the palace was altered so that it could operate as a school. Hence, there is very little left today of what was originally Brocksdorff's Mansion. When the Infantry Cadet Academy moved out in 1788, the navy's young cadets moved in, since the premises were already established as a school. It ought to be mentioned that for a period of time, Hans Christian Andersen lived here in the palace at the home of the head of the naval college, one of the writer's patrons, who had his official residence here. The naval college remained in the palace until 1826. By this time, the mansion had been standing for almost seventy years and had never really been used as a residence, let alone a royal residence.

At this time, Frederik VI, who lived in Schack's Mansion, was about to marry off his youngest daughter, Princess Vilhelmine, to Prince Frederik Carl Christian (the future Frederik VII), the only son of Christian VIII. Thus, Princess Vilhelmine was the groom's second cousin. The King wanted to give the young couple a handsome and fitting home and wanted to renovate Brockdorff's Mansion, which had been a school for more than sixty years and was now worn down. This task was put into the hands of the architect, Jørgen Hansen Koch. Koch had been educated at the Royal Academy of Fine Arts, where he distinguished himself by earning a Gold Medal in 1816. He was already employed in the services of the renowned neo-classicist, C.F. Hansen.

Hence, the palace was decorated in the Empire style, the most distinct signs of which are the very beautiful vestibule and the staircase, flanked by two elegant marble columns in Dorian style. Consequently, the interior of the palace differs markedly from the other three palaces at Amalienborg. The rooms on the ground floor are arranged and decorated as veritable state rooms, especially those facing the garden. The King requested explicitly that there be many rooms on the mezzanine (the uppermost storey). Hence the Gala Room on the *bel étage* facing the palace square could not be equipped with a high ceiling, and consequently the room possesses a rather cozy atmosphere. It was also designed in the Empire style, with lavish and substantial Corinthian pilasters. Jørgen Hansen Koch succeeded in creating a handsome and integral Empire style interior in this palace, and he accomplished this with a speed that is hard to comprehend, even in this day and age, with all our modern technical advances. The palace was finished and ready for the wedding of Crown Prince Frederik and Princess Vilhelmine on November 1, 1828.

The marriage was childless, and moreover, not a happy one. The union was dissolved in 1837. Princess Vilhelmine continued to

live in the palace. In May, 1838 she was remarried in the palace to Duke Karl of Glücksborg. After the wedding, the couple moved to Glücksborg. Meanwhile, following the breakup of his marriage, Crown Prince Frederik had simply had enough of Amalienborg. He lived for many years in Fredericia as the commandant of the Funen Infantry Regiment. From 1848, as sovereign, he went to live at Christiansborg Palace. He was thus the only monarch after Christian VII who did not keep his residence at Amalienborg.

However, it would not be long before the palace was again inhabited by royal residents. Already in 1839, Landgrave Vilhelm of Hessen and his Consort, Princess Louise Charlotte, moved in. Shortly thereafter, they celebrated first the engagement and later on, in 1842, the wedding of their daughter Louise to Prince Christian (later Christian IX). The latter couple eventually attained great popularity as »Europe's parents-in-law«.

In 1869, the palace became the residence of Christian IX's eldest son, Crown Prince Frederik, and his Consort, Princess Lovisa of Sweden. Upon the death of Christian IX in 1906, the Crown Prince ascended to the throne as King Frederik VIII. In keeping with tradition, the King and his very popular Queen continued to maintain their residence in the palace, which thereafter came to be known as Frederik VIII's Pal-

ace. The King's reign was brief. He died in Hamburg in 1912, as a result of heart failure. His widow, Queen Louise (Lovisa), continued to live in the palace, and also at Bernstorff's Castle, until her death in 1926.

On May 24, 1935, Crown Prince Frederik, the oldest son of Christian X, was married in Storkyrkan (the Great Church) in Stockholm to Princess Ingrid, the daughter of the Swedish King, Gustav VI Adolf. The Crown Prince brought home his bride, now Crown Princess Ingrid, to Denmark and the couple took up residence in Frederik VIII's Palace. At the time, however, the palace was not fully renovated and because of this, the Crown Prince and Princess lived for some time in Christian VII's Palace under more or less makeshift conditions. The Crown Princess had Bernadotte blood in her veins, and an artistic sense of colour and exquisite taste. To this very day, the refined interior of the palace bears witness to this. Frederik VIII's Palace became the framework for a rich family life. It was here that all three Princesses, Margrethe, Benedikte and Anne-Marie, were born. In 1947, upon the death of Christian X, Crown Prince Frederik was proclaimed King from the balcony of Christiansborg Palace, and he assumed the throne as King Frederik IX.

As the very model for Danish families, the Royal Family with the three young Princesses succeeded in amal-

gamating a warm and informal humanity with all the dignity we Danes expect of the country's topmost family.

The King died on January 14, 1972. Queen Ingrid continues to live in the palace during the winter months. Frederik VIII's Palace is still the natural gathering site for all of Queen Ingrid's children and grandchildren and their spouses.

The vestibule with the staircase, flanked by two Dorian marble columns. It is the only staircase at Amalienborg created in Empire style. The two statues are by H.V. Bissen: »Diana« and »Echo«.

The central room on the ground floor, facing the garden, is called the
Gobelin Room, after the four Flemish tapestries on the walls.
The room was originally furnished for Prince Frederik Christian,
the later Frederik VII, by Princess Vilhelmine.

The Gala Room with its exquisite neo-Classicist stamp
is so very harmonious largely because the ceiling is lower than in
the Gala Rooms of the other three palaces.
Queen Ingrid has furnished this room as her private living room.

*Just a few years ago, a lift was installed, beautifully
and harmoniously adapted to the building's interior.*

A Chinese lacquered vitrine,
with articles of porcelain.

Queen Ingrid's library. The beautiful and most distinctive chandelier
is Italian. The articles of furniture are Danish,
and were designed by architects Kaare Klint and Ole Wanscher.

Queen Ingrid's study.
On the shelf against the back wall
stands a bust of King Frederik IX.

CHRISTIAN VII'S PALACE

Moltke's Mansion

Representation Chambers and guest apartments   OLE NØRRING

The creation of the Frederikstad and Amalienborg Square was entrusted to the Lord High Chamberlain Adam Gottlob, Count Moltke, who took on the task of serving as director for the project. And thus he was the man who on behalf of the King corresponded with the others who were being offered sites and financial advantages in connection with the construction of their mansions. Naturally, it was Count Moltke who had first choice, and this is why his mansion is the best situated of the four with respect to the incidence of light on the façades and sunshine in the garden. Moltke was the King's absolute favourite. He also happened to be an ingenious and shrewd financier, and was thus in a position to spend much more money than any of the other three patrons on the interior and the fittings in his own mansion.

Moltke's Mansion was the first of the four Amalienborg palaces to be finished. Moltke acquired his deed for the site in May, 1750. In the following year, he held the topping-out ceremony – »with Pomp and Circumstance«. Just three years later, on March 30, 1754, the Lord High Chamberlain was able to inaugurate his mansion with a sumptuous Royal banquet and with the King as guest of honour.

Not only was Moltke a proficient statesman and a financial wizard. He was also a great art-lover and -connoisseur. Very shortly,

Count Moltke's Mansion was filled with fine art, furniture, paintings, tapestries and sculptures. The court architect, Nicolai Eigtved, who was the chief designer of the exteriors of all the palaces, also created the interior of Moltke's Mansion. It was in this mansion, in fact, that Eigtved was given the means to really unfold his talents. What we see here today is a display of some of the most beautiful and unadulterated Rococo that can be found on Danish soil. Eigtved lived just long enough to see the completion of his masterpiece. He died in 1754.

In the following year the architect Nicolas-Henri Jardin came to town, after having spent five years in Rome. He was under the influence of Classicism, especially ancient Roman architecture, and he had worked out a proposal for the Marble Church. When Jardin delivered these plans in 1756, A.G. Moltke sent for the architect to work on the interior of his mansion. Following Moltke's wishes, Jardin designed the magnificent banqueting room, or dining chamber, in the neo-Classicist style preferred and introduced by him. Furthermore, Jardin so elegantly infused touches of neo-Classicism into Eigtved's beautiful Rococo Gala Room that the two entirely divergent styles fit together hand in glove. Finally, Jardin designed the beautiful pavilion in the garden. It was built in a Roman style with a rotunda, two small side wings and a closed

Adam Gottlob,
Count Moltke.

The newly renovated palace with a new sandstone façade and a newly sculpted fronton. The three doorways in the middle leading into the vestibule have been re-painted in the same yellow tone originally used.

After the restoration a plaster cast of Wiedewelt's
»Andromeda« is now displayed in the vestibule's niche.
The original stands in a small pavilion in the
garden at the Glorup estate on Funen,
still owned by the Moltke family.

The vestibule has been re-created after three years of extensive
restoration. The intertwining ciphers of the Queen and the Prince
are inlaid in the marble floor. The decoration for the ciphers was created by
professor Bjørn Nørgaard. The two large lamps, as well as the sconces,
are the work of goldsmith Torben Hardenberg.

gallery behind the rotunda. The pavilion functioned both as garden room and aviary.

There was yet a third architect who would come to leave his mark on the palace. The young Caspar Frederik Harsdorff returned to Denmark in 1764 after having been educated abroad. On Moltke's commission, Harsdorff designed, in the central space on the ground floor with access to the garden, an elegant and dignified room for Count Moltke's second wife, Sophie Hedevig Moltke, whom the Count married shortly after the death of his first wife in 1760.

The owner himself died in 1792. His son, Joachim Godske Moltke, was already a land-owner and was now about to inherit Bregent-

ved as well as the mansion. The inheritance of Bregentved, how-ever, saddled the younger Moltke with so many financial obligati-ons that he considered selling off the mansion at Amalienborg. As fate would have it, such considerations were to be short-lived.

On a cold wintry night in 1794, the night between the 26th and the 27th of February, Copenhagen was illuminated by the blazing glow of a conflagration. Christiansborg Castle was burning. The Royal Family was without a roof over their heads. The idea of look-ing in the direction of Amalienborg immediately suggested itself as Moltke's Mansion was, in fact, for sale. On March 5, the mansion was purchased, with all the furnishings except for the collection of paintings, for the sum of 45,000 rigsdaler and the King, Christian VII, moved in right away. One week later, the neighbouring build-ing, Schack's Mansion (the present-day residence palace), was pur-chased for the Crown Prince and his family. In comparison with the enormous Christiansborg Castle, the spatial conditions in Moltke's Palace, which was now named »The King's Palace« (later on it came to be called Christian VII's Palace), were quite cramped. In order to create more space, the magnificently columned vesti-bule in the ground floor's central ressault with direct access from the palace square was demolished after a few years. The floor was then elevated so that it became level with the surrounding rooms and Harsdorff, the architect, thereby created space for two addi-tional rooms as well as several rooms in the basement.

Prior to this, the marble terraces situated between the palace itself and the pavilions had been roofed over, thus incorporating

the pavilions in the palace. At the same time, the colonnade was constructed in order to establish quick and easy access from the palace of the Crown Prince to that of the King. Traditionally, the entire Royal Family would eat two meals together every day, lunch and »Royal table« (the evening meal). At the suggestion of the Lord High Cham-berlain of the day, A.W. Hauch, and the Crown Prince, Harsdorff was entrusted with the task of building the colonnade between the two palaces. Since no one ever really thought the structure would be standing for long, and seeing that money was scarce – large sums had been used on the repair of the Crown Prince's palace – the colonnade was built of wood. However, the colonnade is still standing, and it has become an integral part of Amalienborg. Certainly, Saly's equestrian statue is at its handsomest when viewed framed by the colonnade!

In 1808, Christian VII died. On March 16, 1808, from the bal-cony of Christian VII's Palace, the Crown Prince was proclaimed King Frederik VI. As regent, Frederik continued to live in Schack's Mansion. Ever since, it has been the tradition that the new monarch continues to reside in the palace that has been his or her residence as heir to the throne.

Since the death of Christian VII, this palace has never again been the residence palace. It has served, by turns, as representation chambers, residence for Court functionaries and office area. In 1853, after a great tug-of-war, the Foreign Ministry was allotted the uppermost storey (the mezzanine) and most of the bel étage and continued to keep its headquarters in Christian VII's Palace until 1885. The second Christiansborg Castle burned down in 1884 and along with it, the royal representation premises were destroyed. Once again, everyone looked in the direction of Ama-lienborg, and specifically at Christian VII's Palace. The Foreign Ministry was then re-located to Levetzau's Mansion (the present Christian VIII's Palace) and Christian VII's Palace was quickly overhauled. Since that time, it has been used exclusively as a guest and representation palace.

For almost a century, the palace lay dormant, without any sig-nificant maintenance projects, apart from certain conversions made

The main staircase with its exquisite Rococo stucco. The stair-carpet was designed by the Queen and with its golden hues leads from the cool-coloured vestibule up to the Gala Room's gilded stucco and wood-carvings. At the foot of the stairs stands a model of Saly's equestrian statue.

at the end of the nineteen-thirties when central heating was installed in all four of the Amalienborg palaces.

In the 1970s, the palace was shored up with a new foundation and an extensive restoration of the façade was planned by the Palaces and Properties Agency. However, no means were set aside for a restoration of the interior, which was badly in need of repair. Nor did the palace live up to the demands of our time for a guest palace. However, private donors lent a hand. A committee, »The Palace Committee« – with representatives from the largest business organizations, the Palaces and Properties Agency and the Court – was established. The committee collected more than seventeen million Danish crowns. With this sum and, especially, with the appurtenant moral support, the Finance Committee granted the means for a thorough restoration. The planning was implemented by the Palaces and Properties Agency.

The single person who has exerted the greatest influence on the interior of the palace, however, is the Queen herself. From the very outset, her Majesty the Queen has participated in the amplification of every single detail, and the interiors, with curtains and furniture, and the paintings and the carpets, all bear the distinct stamp of the Queen's unerring sense of colour and refined taste. It is precisely this that has given the palace its very intimate and personal cachet. It is a home – albeit a very aristocratic home.

The renovated palace was inaugurated on the Queen's birthday in 1996. Upon the inauguration it was decided by Her Majesty the Queen that, until further notice, the palace would be opened to the public for brief periods, with guided tours.

The Perseus Chamber takes its name from the Flemish tapestries
that have adorned the room since the palace was erected.
They tell the tale from Greek mythology of Perseus, who rescues
Andromeda from mortal danger.
Here, the shackled Andromeda and her terror-stricken father
are seen.

The wedding feast of Andromeda and Perseus, after Perseus has saved Andromeda's life.

The entry into Argos, where Perseus's grandfather was the reigning king.

Splendid tapestries woven at Beauvais, after a painting by
François Boucher, decorate the walls of the Chinese saloon.
The tapestries with Chinese motifs were a gift to Count Moltke
from King Louis XV of France.

*The Velvet Chamber features newly woven velvet tapestries
made at the very same mill in Lyon that executed the
weaving of the original tapestries in the 1750s, which were
a gift to Count Moltke from Louis XV.*

The Picture Gallery appears today almost as it did during the time of Christian VII except for the fact that the stove-niches are fitted today as vitrines containing part of the Sevres-service which Louis XV presented to Christian VII during his visit to Paris in 1768. The carpets were made in France after old Aubusson patterns. They are a gift to the Queen from Tom's factories and the Danish Employers Confederation.

The Gala Room is the palace's most magnificent room.
It constitutes the finest example of Eigtved's Rococo decoration.
The later neo-Classicist modifications executed by the architect
Jardin fit beautifully into the interior.

Detail from the Gala Room. The paintings above the two fireplaces and the five overdoors were painted by François Boucher as allegorical pictures representing the sciences and the arts. »The Allegory of Music« is seen here.

The Gala Room facing Amalienborg Palace Square. The silk curtains with embroidered roses were made in Paris as copies of the originals. In the Gala Room, the great Royal banquets (dinner parties) are held, among them the traditional New Year's banquet.

*On the left: A peek through a suite of rooms
leading into the Gala Room.*

*The Banqueting Room was designed by the architect Jardin
in the entire depth of the palace, in what had previously
been two rooms. It is Denmark's first neo-Classicist interior
and constitutes a beautiful example of Jardin's capacities.*

The five octagonal paintings mounted in the ceiling were taken from the pavilion with the golden orbs in Rosenborg Garden. They were painted in the 1660s by Karel van Mander and depict jovial folksy scenes. The paintings are encircled by gilded stucco representing clams, seaweed and conches, all of which refer to the room's original function as a natural history cabinet.

The table is set for a luncheon in the Rose Room. At the initiative of the Queen this room, after its restoration, provides the setting for a grand display of the Flora Danica service.

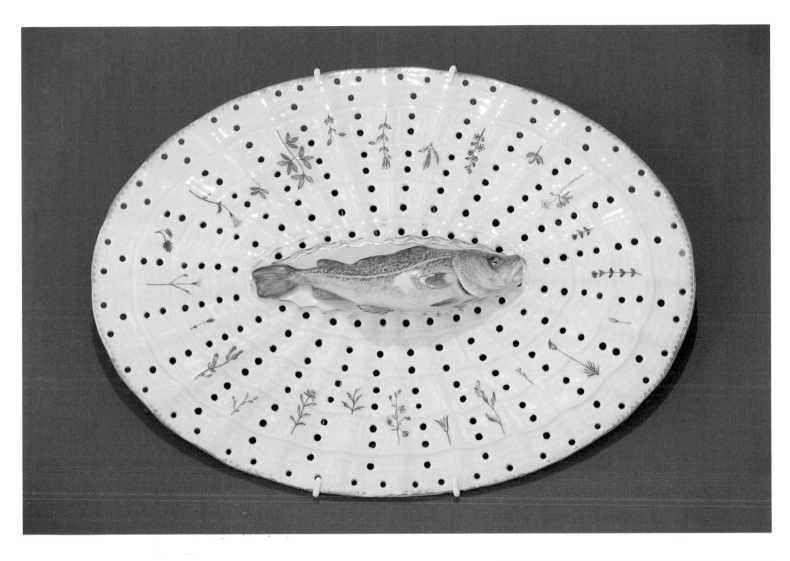

Flora Danica:

Flower basket with modeled flowers. Knife handles, gathered six by six.

Platter with modeled flowers.

Grated fish platter.

Pierced ice dome. In 1803, four pieces were produced. All of them are intact.

The Flora Danica service was manufactured by the Royal Danish Porcelain
Factory after the illustrations found on the plates in the scientific work
entitled »Flora Danica«. Production began in the late 1780s.
Exactly when is not known with certainty. It was discontinued in 1802.
All in all, the original Flora Danica service numbered 1802 pieces,
of which 1530 are still intact.

Flora Danica plates.

The King's Saloon. Certain pieces of regal furniture are on loan from the National Historical Museum at Frederiksborg, such as this beautiful inlaid bureau.

The overdoors in Harsdorff's Chamber, painted
by Mandelberg and depicting four reclining muses,
supplanted Pilo's original overdoors when
Harsdorff re-designed the room.

Harsdorff's Chamber was designed for Count Moltke's second wife around 1770 by the architect Harsdorff, who removed every smidgen of Rococo and replaced it with painted decorations on a golden ground, featuring neo-Classicist motifs.

The interior of Harsdorff's Cabinet, adjacent to Harsdorff's Chamber, stands today as an utterly charming room in nuances of blue. The miniature paintings have been executed on copper plates and represent Swedish kings and queens.

The toilet-tray and -box of gilded silver from a 28-piece gilded silver set, which belonged to Frederik VIII's Queen, Louise (Lovisa), was created in Berlin between 1821 and 1841 by the firm of Johann George Hossauer, presumably after a prototype by Karl Friedrich Schinkel. Earlier on, the set was kept in the Garden Saloon in Frederik VIII's Palace.

Gilded writing set.

The objects shown on this page are only a few of the many splendid stately objects that are set out when the palace is occupied by guests.

Detail from Moltke's bedroom with the dressing table and
Moltke's bust against the back wall.

Moltke's bedroom. The bed of state is a faithful copy of Count
Moltke's original bed, which is found today at Bregentved.

On the left: *A serving tray and trays for odds and ends created by H.M. the Queen with beautiful paper cutouts, découpages. Trays and baskets of this kind have been placed in all the guest rooms.*

»Genuine pearls sow no doubt.« »La Pureté des Perles – ne se doute pas«. Everyone of the Queen's découpages tells a story – a fairy-tale.

THE PALACE GARDENS

Behind Christian VII's Palace

In 1749 King Frederik V asked the court architect Nicolai Eigtved to draw up a town plan for the Frederikstad, which subsequently and over a great number of years came to be built by a number of different building entrepreneurs. However, the overall impression is one of unity. This can be attributed largely to the efforts of Lord High Chamberlain Adam Gottlob Moltke, who in keeping with his agreement with the King called upon some of the realm's very best men, General Christian Levetzau, Privy Councillor Severin Løvenskiold and Baron Joachim Brockdorff, each to build – along with Moltke himself – a mansion according to common guidelines. The sites were then placed at the disposal of the four builders – free of charge – and the four men were also granted tax exemptions for a period of thirty years.

This is the reason why the four mansions, each with its own back garden, were built according to identical plans, and constitute a square in the very hub of the Frederikstad. (See the aerial photo on page 13.) In connection with the recently completed palace restorations, the garden behind Christian VII's Palace has been designed to appear as a visual re-creation of the original garden layout, as seen from a bird's eye view.

The garden was idyllically laid out between two cobblestone-paved courtyard areas. The first one, facing Frederiksgade, was a stable yard with enough room for a score of horses and depots for the coaches. The other one, facing Amaliegade, was a kitchen yard, containing a wash house, a woodshed and the large kitchen which, through the basement in the castle, was to serve Royalty and guests on festive occasions.

In its day, the garden was stocked with an abundance of espaliers and several shady avenues of lime trees leading to the garden pavilion and volière. When the palace, which was uninhabited for a number of years, was restored, many of these species were not planted again. The aim was rather to reproduce the essential structure of Eigtved's garden while maintaining a reasonable economic

point of view. The parterre in front of the stairway of the palace and the sunken lawns so characteristic for the time around 1750-70 have been re-created.

The pavilion was erected in 1760 by Jardin, almost ten years after the mansion and the garden were put into use. He designed the building in the style of early Classicism as a domed pavilion with a columned rotunda and – following the express wishes of his client, A.G. Moltke – with two aviaries for beautiful and exotic birds.

Large bird cages manifest as independent buildings are well known in many cultures. In China, there are examples going all the way back to the 12th century BC. In Europe, the Roman builder, Marcus Terentius Varro (116-27 BC), gave some of the earliest known instructions for the construction of a volière as well as advice on how to provide water, air and light ... »but not too many large windows, for the sense of privation that the sight of living trees and free-flying birds might arouse in the caged creatures will make them pine away and die.«

With the construction of the two aviaries, fashioned according to Varro's instructions, the entire pavilion-building emerged as a small gem of grace and beauty. The pavilion has not yet been restored. Were this to be done, yet another beautiful memento from bygone days would come to life.

Two zinc figures have been placed very decoratively in the middle of the garden. Originally, the statues were part of the roof on top of Christian VII's Palace, but they were removed from their high position because of weathering and subsequently put in storage until Queen Margrethe decided that it might be a good idea to place them in the newly restored garden. When the castle was built, these figures were originally carved in wood, but the wind and the weather caused the wood to rot, which is why they were re-created in zinc. The zinc did not fare much better in the harsh Danish weather, and the figures now sitting and standing on the balustrades of the palaces have been carved in limestone.

Christian VII's Palace
as seen from the
newly restored garden.

The pavilion was
built as a circular
temple. It is used as a
tea pavilion and contains
two aviaries. It is a
shady sanctuary with a
view to the garden and
the palace.

The cherubs of zinc were taken down from the balustrade of Christian VII's Palace due to weathering and have been given a new life in the palace garden by Queen Margrethe.

The circular pavilion, as seen from the avenue of lime trees and the palace stairs.

The sunken lawn, for playing petanque or other ball games, is characteristic of the time between 1750 and 1770.

The triangular parterre in front of the palace stairs.

CHRISTIAN VIII'S PALACE

Levetzau's Mansion

Residence of Crown Prince Frederik and
The Royal Danish Collections

GERDA PETRI

Christian VIII's Palace has twice been the residence of a monarch. The first time was during the reign of Christian VIII, from 1839 until 1848, when Prince Christian Frederik as the closest living male relative of the Oldenborg line succeeded Frederik VI, who had two daughters but no sons. Christian VIII had been living in the palace since the tender age of eight when after the fire of Christiansborg in 1794 he moved into Amalienborg with his siblings and parents, the Heir Presumptive Frederik and his wife, Princess Sofie Frederikke of Mecklenburg-Schwerin. The Heir Presumptive was the son of King Frederik V and Queen Juliane Marie.

Following the wishes of the Heir Presumptive, the artist Nicolai Abraham Abildgaard (1743-1809) was entrusted with the task of converting what had been the Levetzau Mansion into a residence for a royal family. Approximately seventy-five of the artist's watercolour sketches for the ornamentation of the palace are found today in the Royal Collection of Prints and Drawings. When a series of extensive renovations was carried out at the end of the 1980s, some of the interiors of the palace were partially re-created on the basis of these sketches.

Abildgaard's interior was an expression of the new taste of the times. As a reaction to the Rococo's asymmetry and twining lines, it was the ancient and classic ideals – with columns, pilasters, straight lines and thorough symmetry – that now came to the fore. This was different from what the original style of the palace complex had been but it was executed with a prescience from the hand of the artist at which posterity can only marvel. The crown jewel of the work was the Gala Room, a truly splendid vision of international format – meriting a journey. What was characteristic of Abildgaard, moreover, was his intrepid combination of the colours which were the fashion of the day in Europe's trend-setting spheres.

Frederik, the Heir Presumptive, died in 1805. Subsequently, his son, Prince Christian Frederik (Christian VIII) took over the palace where, interrupted only by sojourns abroad, he lived for the rest of his life. His only child, Prince Frederik Carl Christian (the later King Frederik VII), the offspring from Prince Christian Frederik's first marriage to his cousin Charlotte Frederikke of Mecklenburg-Schwerin, was born in the southern section of the *bel étage* facing Frederiksgade. Later, in 1836, in the very same wing, Prince Christian Frederik commissioned painters G.C. Hilker, H. Eddelien and C. Købke to decorate a Pompeiian-inspired bedroom for his second Consort, Princess Caroline Amalie of Augustenborg.

In the adjoining chamber, Queen Caroline Amalie, in 1852 – after Christian VIII had died – had a library built in a neo-Gothic style. This style never appealed to Danish taste but it was certainly popular in Russia, Germany and England and during this period was frequently employed in the interior design of libraries. The room's architect was Chr. V. Nielsen, a student of G.F. Hetsch, while the master joiner P.L. Wolff and the wood-carver H.V. Brinkopff were responsible for the furniture. The library was a gift to the nation from the Queen Dowager, in commemoration of the childless Royal Couple.

Abildgaard's Gala Room, the Reception Room, Throne Room and Blue Cabinet, the Pompeiian Chamber, the Gothic Library and the two new Order of Chivalry chambers, furnished according to suggestions put forth by Her Majesty Queen Margrethe II, were all part of the aforementioned renovation, accomplished at the end of the 1980s. The renovation was funded by the Palaces and Properties Agency, a department of the Ministry of Housing which administers the royal castles. Following the wishes of the Queen, the *bel étage* has now been opened to the public, through regularly scheduled guided tours conducted by The Royal Danish Collections, situated on the ground floor of this palace.

Christian VIII was interested in art. And he was a collector. During his reign, from 1839 until 1848, he employed in his services a museum curator to care for his outstanding collection of ancient vases, which were displayed on the ground floor. The col-

*Christian VIII's palace, built by Privy Councillor Christian
Frederik Levetzau. In 1794, after the destruction
by fire of Christiansborg Castle, the palace was bought by the
Heir Presumptive, Prince Frederik.*

The royal staircase leading to the newly restored Abildgaard-saloons and the residence of the present Crown Prince.

lection was opened to those who were especially interested. The appearance of these study tours meant that for the first time in Denmark ancient ceramics were included in the university curriculum.[1] The private study chamber of the absolute monarch himself was a rather unpretentious room facing the palace square with a view of Saly's equestrian statue. The room itself is still intact and is now part of the Amalienborg Museum's permanent exhibition.

Following the death of Christian VIII in 1848, the Queen Dowager remained in the palace until her demise in 1881. For the next seventeen years, until 1898, the premises were used by the Foreign Ministry and other administrative organs.

In 1912, the palace became the royal residence for the second time. In 1898, as he was about to marry Princess Alexandrine of Mecklenburg-Schwerin, even before he became Crown Prince, Prince Christian (the later King Christian X) was given the palace as a residence by his grandfather, King Christian IX. At that time, and once again on the occasion of the couple's silver wedding anniversary, the palace was reconditioned and modernized. The completion of the new Christiansborg Palace did not compel the Royal Couple to change residence. They continued to live in the palace at Amalienborg for the rest of their lives. Thus, Amalienborg's function as a royal residence was definitively sealed.

During the reign of King Christian X, the palace was the scene of epoch-making historic and dramatic moments: the enfranchisement of women in 1915; the Easter Crisis in 1920, and in the same year, the reunion of North Schleswig and Denmark; and the Second World War, from 1940 until 1945 – events for which the King is remembered, events about which he made up his mind in his study, which can still be seen here.

Following the passing of the Royal Couple, the Heir Presumptive Knud took over the palace. The weddings of both Prince Ingolf and Prince Christian, the sons of Knud and his Princess, Caroline-Mathilde, were held here.

With the most recent renovations, state apartments and a shared bachelor apartment for Crown Prince Frederik and Prince Joachim were established. It is still the home of the Crown Prince, whereas Prince Joachim has moved his Amalienborg quarters into another part of the building, following his wedding to Princess Alexandra. Moreover, premises for the Queen's Reference Library have been established in the pavilion facing the Marble Church.

On the occasion of the abovementioned series of renovations, the greater part of the ground floor was converted to house a permanent extension of The Royal Danish Collections at Rosenborg.

On the sixteenth of April, 1994, her birthday, Her Majesty the Queen officially opened the new Amalienborg museum. As in the days of Christian VIII, the palace came to provide a framework for museum functions, only this time, more extrovertedly and even more community oriented. The extension of the Rosenborg Collection is concentrated around The House of Glücksborg and around more recent royal history. Prince Christian (King Christian IX), who in 1863 succeeded the last of the Oldenborg line, the childless Frederik VII, was the first regent of the house of Glücksborg. The Prince was not the son of a king, but his father, Duke Wilhelm Holsten-Beck of Glücksborg, was indeed a descendant of Christian I, and his mother, Princess Louise Caroline of Hessen, was a granddaughter of Frederik V.

Already in the 1950s, it was King Frederik IX and Queen Ingrid's idea that the Rosenborg Collection, which had been suffering since the last century from a lack of room for the display of more recent royal history, should be allowed to expand into Christian IX's Palace (at present Queen Margrethe's Palace). The thought occurred because in our own century it seems a natural thing to regard the line of kings and queens as one continuous sequence from Christian I until the present day. An exhibitional separation between the House of Oldenborg and the House of Glücksborg would thus no longer provoke political unrest, as it might have done in the previous century, when the shift from the royal branch of Oldenborg to that of Glücksborg brought about historical conflicts.[2]

The plans, however, were first put into effect much later, when in 1977-1982, on the basis of sketches by Queen Ingrid, a somewhat smaller museum was established in Christian IX's Palace.

The Royal Danish Collections at Rosenborg have been open to the public since 1838. At that time, arranging the royal study-chambers in chronological sequence and displaying the rooms so as to suggest that the King had just left the premises was something new indeed. It was also something of a novelty that the Kings Frederik VI, Christian VIII and Frederik VII were represented very shortly after their deaths with the display of the interiors of their personal chambers. By this means, the exhibition became something more than a mirror of the past. It also became a part of contemporary history. The exhibition aroused a great deal of international interest. Subsequently, both the principle of exhibiting interiors and the desire to put contemporary history on display have been incorporated into the exhibition politics of museums.

After the cessation of the absolute monarchy and the institution of the Danish Constitution in 1849, the Collection's intimate connection with the Royal House continued to be a vital one. Contrary to the other royal art collections which were transferred on the abovementioned occasion into state ownership, the Collection at Rosenborg became a royal entailed estate, making it inheritable from one sovereign to the next, with its own Board of Directors, where both the state and the Royal Family are represented. This status differentiates the Collection from the national museums.

In the establishment of the museum at Amalienborg, the above exhibition principles have naturally been continued. The permanent exhibition includes interiors from the first four generations of the House of Glücksborg: Christian IX's study, Queen Louise's drawing room, and the studies of Frederik VIII and Christian X. In consultation with both Queen Margrethe and Queen Ingrid, King Frederik IX's study was re-created in connection with the centennial celebration of the King in 1999. Moreover, the museum contains an introductory room with family portraits, a genealogical room with a detailed survey of the royal blood-lines and family connections from 1863 until 1998, The Jewel Room, a costume collection and Christian X and Queen Alexandrine's private dining room. The same Royal Couple's spacious garden saloon, with the only extant original Rococo ceiling in the palace, is also on view. This garden saloon and an adjacent room are used for the presentation of special exhibitions revolving around royal culture, then and now.

The core of the permanent exhibition is the constellation of Christian IX's study and Queen Louise's drawing room. These rooms were left untouched at Amalienborg through the 1940s. During the reign of King Frederik IX and Queen Ingrid, they were inventoried by the National Museum and transferred into the Collections. Both interiors are fully intact. Everything here is original, from the curtains, the portières and the carpets to the many articles standing here exactly as they did during the times of the Royal Couple. The rooms have been transferred from Christian IX's Palace, where the present-day Royal Couple resides. A few minor deviations in the spatial dimensions of the room have entailed certain minor changes in the arrangements.

The first Royal Couple of the Glücksborg line achieved an enormous degree of popularity in their own day, primarily on account of their intense family life. In a masterly way – perhaps it was the Queen's doing – all six of the children were married to royalty. Special status was afforded by the marriages between the oldest Princess, Alexandra, and the future Edward VII of England, in 1863, and between the somewhat younger Princess Dagmar and the future Russian Czar Alexander III, in 1866. In 1869, the Crown Prince, the future Frederik VIII, was married to the Swedish King's daughter Lovisa of Sweden-Norway. The younger Prince, Vilhelm, was elected King of Greece in 1863 under the name of Georg and in 1867 he married the Grand Duchess Olga of Russia. Later on, the two youngest children were also married off: Princess Thyra was married in 1878 to the Crown Prince of Hannover, Duke Ernst August of Cumberland, and Prince Valdemar wed Princess Marie of Orléans in 1885. All these marriages gave luster to the nation, and the Royal Couple became widely known as »Europe's in-laws«.

The many international connections did not prevent the children, the grandchildren and the children in-law from flocking home regularly to »Angel-mama« and »Angel-papa« at the Amalienborg, Bernstorff and Fredensborg palaces. There are a great many mementoes in the museum attesting to this. One effect of the intimate family ties was that the childhood home at Amalienborg was not split up when the Royal Couple died. Queen Louise died first in 1898. When King Christian IX died in 1906, the children and their spouses resolved that the home should remain unchanged, so that they could all continue to resort to their accustomed nest.

The decision to keep the family hearth intact subsequently proved to be of benefit to the exiled Empress Dagmar when she came back to Denmark after the outbreak of the Russian Revolution. Up until her death in 1928, Dagmar spent her winter months in the familiar surroundings at Amalienborg. After this time, the home was left untouched.

Their awareness of this royal residence that had fallen into a Sleeping Beauty-like slumber for a whole generation was the incentive for Frederik IX and Queen Ingrid's decision that some of these rooms should devolve upon The Royal Danish Collections and remain at Amalienborg. Fully cognizant of the home's cultural and historical value, the National Museum in 1948 was assigned the task of making a thorough inventory and photographic rendering of the entire home.[3] This exact documentation was used by The Royal Danish Collections in re-mounting the two interiors.

As opposed to Christian X's room, which is displayed in its original location, Frederik VIII's study is a reconstruction. The room was originally created in 1869 in Frederik VIII's Palace, later to become the residence of King Frederik IX and Queen Ingrid. The reconstruction has taken place in connection with the establishment of the museum and has been executed with the aid of photographs from around 1894 and the original list of inventory. The imitation gilt leather tapestry covering the walls has been executed manually after the rediscovered original embossing stone and the curtains have been made from remnants of the original material. The furniture was made in 1869 in a neo-Renaissance style which was so prominent at the time, especially for use in a gentleman's study or library because it provided a dark and serious atmosphere thought to be in keeping with masculinity. Here is an example of how the time made use of traditional stylistic features for the purpose of accentuating the room's function and for indicating whether the primary occupant was female or male.

With the Amalienborg Museum's placement in Christian VIII's Palace, the public is afforded the opportunity of entering a 17th-century royal palace where a number of interiors and a great many articles cast a light over the everyday life of royalty. The royal milieu is an elitist minority, but as a cultural prototype, it has exerted a far-reaching effect. Up until the present century, it was inside the houses of royalty that new cultural standards were first accepted. Later on, these spread to other layers in the society. At the same time, the royal milieu constitutes a place where norms and traditions are safeguarded and sheltered from change.

1 Lund, John: »Sans og Samling: Christian VIII's oldsagserhvervelser fra Tunesien, Grækenland og Paris« [Aptitude and Collection: archaeological acquisitions from Tunesia, Greece and Paris] by C.T. Falbe in »Christian VIII og Nationalmuseet« [Christian VIII and the National Museum], 1999.

2 Boesen, G. »Rosenborgs nye annex på Amalienborg« [Rosenborg's New Annex at Amalienborg], Gutenberghus 1977.

3 Clemmensen, T. and Mackeprang, M.B.: »Christian IX's Palæ på Amalienborg 1750-1906« [Christian IX's Palace at Amalienborg, 1750-1906], Gyldendal 1956.

Flora hovers gracefully on a wall in the Pompeiian-inspired sleeping chamber, which Christian VIII – a devotee of classical antiquity – had arranged in 1836. Here was a style favoured by the aristocracy of the day as well as the artistic circles. At the time, the central impulse emanated from the sculptor Hermann Ernst Freund, who had implemented this style in his own home. The decoration was painted by H. Eddelien, G.C. Hilker and C. Købke.

The Violet Audience Chamber. Heir Presumptive Frederik selected Nicolai Abildgaard for the task of transforming the palace. This choice was profoundly original, because Abildgaard was well-known as a painter, but had rarely worked as an architect.

Nicolai Abildgaard's neo-Classicist Gala Room, created for music, dancing and festivities – constitutes a reaction to the earlier Rococo's scrolled, asymmetric decorations. The two statues representing the muses of dance and flute-playing, Terpsichore and Euterpe, are early works of the renowned Bertel Thorvaldsen. Many people still remember King Christian X waving to the crowds on the Palace Square from the balcony of this elegant room.

The neo-Gothic library of the Queen Dowager, Caroline Amalie.
The room was designed by the architect Chr.V. Nielsen in 1852. The furniture
was built by master joiner P.L. Wolff and wood-carver H.V. Brinkopff. On the five
carved columns there are busts of the day's cultural luminaries: B.S. Ingemann,
A. Oehlenschläger, N.F.S. Grundtvig, A.S. Ørsted and I.P. Mynster.
The library was used assiduously by the Queen and her female acquaintances
for literary meetings. A frequent guest was the great author of the day,
Hans Christian Andersen.

The stylistic blend apparent in Queen Louise's private quarters from the 1890s is typical of the day's feminine rooms; here is an admixture of Victorian and neo-Rococo. However, the light-colored articles of furniture, which were re-upholstered on the occasion of the Royal Couple's golden wedding anniversary in 1892, suggest that at the time the royal court was on its way toward new trends in the field of residential design; the furniture of the day's bourgeoisie was typically covered with dark-coloured upholstery.

Photos and knick-knacks by the hundreds surrounded Christian IX, the first of the Glücksborg line, in his study, where the desks of both the King and the cabinet secretary were situated.

The enormous quantity of items indicates that it certainly was »the time of many hands«, when the availability of labour for dusting and cleaning a room was taken as a given.

Frederik VIII's study was fitted up in 1869, when the newly wedded Crown Prince and Princess moved into Frederik VIII's Palace. At the time, everything in this room was new and a manifestation of the fact that the combination of traditional craftsmanship and new technology made it possible to simulate, for example, Renaissance furniture, weapons and gilt leather.
The design of this room signaled the newest trend and became a prototype for a gentleman's study for decades to come.

Christian X's study testifies to the King's interest in the military. In addition to a wall-sized shield with different types of weapons, there are vases, candlesticks and other fixtures made from parts of weapons. A number of symbols speak of the King's nationalistic sentiments: flags, a stone from the Dannevirke, the hoof from the white horse the King rode at the occasion of the reunion with North Schleswig in 1920, a narwhal's tusk from Greenland and a bust of Holger Danske. The atmosphere present in the room can be found in the studies of many middle-class gentlemen in succeeding generations. The crammed writing table does not leave much room for writing; this seems to be characteristic of the male rulers of the Glücksborg line.

Frederik IX's study. The room is characterized by a choice selection of exquisite Danish cabinetwork dating from the middle of the present century. In keeping with his forefathers, this King also enjoyed surrounding himself with photographs of family and friends. Music was a vital necessity for Frederik IX. The presence of the grand piano attests to this.

THE AMALIEGARDEN

The public palace park on the waterfront   KJELD RASMUSSEN

In the years when the Frederikstad was being planned, and until very recently, the waterfront running along Toldbodgade served as the storage yard for lumber coming into Copenhagen by sea transport. Over the years, the waterfront area with its inflammable stock was built up and developed haphazardly, except for the area situated adjacent to Amalienborg Palace. Building consortia and government authorities could never agree on a mutually acceptable plan that could be adapted in a natural way to the palace milieu.

In 1980, the shipbuilder Mærsk Mc-Kinney Møller and his wife took an initiative. With funds made available for the purpose by the foundation, »A.P. Møller and Hustru Chastine Mc-Kinney Møllers Fond«, the site was purchased. With international foresight, a project proposal was developed by the Belgian landscape architect, Jean Dologne, in collaboration with the Italian sculptor, Arnaldo Pomodoro, who has created the large central fountain, the four sculptural pillars and the two side-fountains. It was the foundation's wish to create a plan that would finally solve the problem surrounding the »Klondike« that was emerging in the not yet organized area adjacent to Amalienborg.

At the park's consecration in 1983, Amaliehaven was transferred officially to state ownership and to the city of Copenhagen as a gift. With this act, the foundation's vision was brought to realization in the most beautiful way. A.P. Møller, Denmark's most prominent

international shipbuilder and business entrepreneur, has thus become the greatest Danish contributor to Amalienborg, with his underwriting of both the establishment of Amaliehaven and the renovation of Saly's equestrian statue on the palace square.

Every year, more than 100,000 guests come to visit Amaliehaven and Amalienborg Square. The garden naturally assumes its role as an integral element in the palace complex, with its very own style and great aesthetic qualities. The directrices in the structure of the garden draw the visitor into a green oasis in the midst of the city. The garden's architectonic plan – open toward the waterfront and closed off to Toldbodgade by a wall – provides a discreet screening for the private residences of the Royal Family in the two buildings, Christian IX's and Frederik VIII's Palaces.

As you approach Amalienborg Square from the waterside, the fountain in the center connects Amalienborg Square, the Marble Church and the waterfront into one magnificent experience.

The scheme of the garden comprises 121 different kinds of bushes and trees. Moreover, there are a large number of perennials, and the profusion of flowers changes with the seasons. Amaliehaven has its very own style and a genuineness – adapted to the atmosphere of the spot – and an elegant simplicity which makes it an oasis for busy city people and for the tourists who come to visit.

Arnaldo Pomodoro has created this bubbling fountain, framed by the four distinctive pillars - each of which measures several meters in height and glitters like gold in the sunlight.

Previous page: One of the two side-fountains which terminate the garden at either end. Unique bronze reliefs with stylized suns, sprayed by a cascade of falling water.

Amaliehaven's effervescent fountain unifies the universal elements of water, sky and sunshine into a fabulous experience in ever-constant flux.

A vista from the waterfront across Amaliehaven's central fountain toward Frederik's Church or, as it is more commonly known, the Marble Church.

Amaliehaven binds the palace and the waterfront together into an aggregate whole, offering intimate and cozy places
of refuge and viewpoints with grandiose vistas over the garden and the Sound.
The flowers in the park change with the seasons. Above, a flowering cherry tree in the sunlight of the spring. Below, Copen-
hageners and tourists, enjoying the sunshine and the view as they sit on the garden's long stone bench on the waterfront.

Historic sailing vessels from all over the world anchor here on the waterfront.

The garden's architecture and ground plan – open toward the waterfront and closed off with a high wall toward Toldbodgade – provide a discreet screening off from the Royal Family's residences.

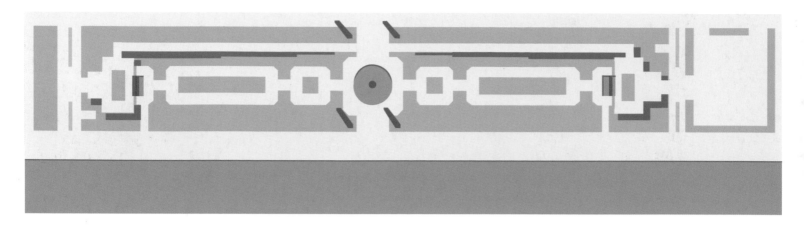

LIST OF PLANTS IN AMALIEHAVEN

PROVIDED BY THE PALACES AND PROPERTIES AGENCY

Achillea filipendulina »Schwellenburg«
Acer campestre
Acer ginnala
Acer pensylvanicum
Acer platanoides »Globulosum«
Acer platanoides »Globulosum«, bush
Alchemilla mollis
Alnus glutinosa
Anaphalis triplinervis
Anemone jap. »Honorine de Jobert«
Anemone silvestris
Amelanchier laevis
Aralia elata
Aronia melanocarpa »Hugin«
Aster amellus »Dwarf King«
Astilbe ssp.
Berberis juliana
Berberis candidula
Berberis thunbergii
Berberis verrucosa
Bergenia cordifolia
Bergenia cordifolia »Silberlicht«
Buddleja alternifolia
Buxus sempervirens »Handsworthi-
    ensis«
Calamintha nepeta ssp. nepeta
Carpinus betulus, hedge
Carpinus betulus »Monumentalis«
Carpinus betulus »Fastigiata«
Caryopteris incana
Chaenomeles japonica
Cimicifuga simplex »Brunette«
Cornus alba »Argentomarginata«
Cornus alba »Sibirica«
Cornus alba
Cornus sericea »Flaviramea«
Cotoneaster dammerii
Cotoneaster dammerii »Skogholm«
Cotoneaster dielsiana
Crataegus crus-galli

Crataegus clorosarca Tilia sp.
Crataegus prunifolia
Deutzia gracilis
Dictamnus albus »Albiflorus«
Dictamnus albus var. caucasicus
Ephedra distachya
Epimedium rubrum
Euonymus alata
Euonymus fortunei »Emerald
    Gaity«
Euonymus fortunei »Emerald
    Gold«
Euonymus fortunei »Nyrans«
Euonymus fortunei »Vegetus«
Forsythia intermedia »Lynwood«
Fraxinus ornus
Geranium endr. »Rose Clair«
Geranium »Johnson's Blue«
Geranium macrorrhizum »Album«
Geranium platypetalum
Geranium renardii
Geranium sanguineum »Album«
Ginkgo biloba
Gypsophila repens »Rosenschleier«
Hedera helix
Hedera helix »Hibernica«
Hemerocallis flava
Hippophae rhamnoides
Hosta plantaginea »Honey Bells«
Hosta ventricosa
Hydrangea anomala petiolaris
Hydrangea »Blue Wave«
Hydrangea paniculata
Hypericon calycinum
Iberis sempervirens
Ilex aquifolium
Jasminum nudiflorum
Juniperus communis »Hibernica«
Kerria japonica
Lathyrus vernus

Lavandula angustifolia
Lavandula angustifolia »Munstead«
Ligustrum obtusifolium »Regeli«
Ligustrum ovalifolium »Aureum«
Lilium candidum
Lonicera pileata
Lysimachia nummularia
Mahonia aquifolium »Aqu«
Malus sargentii
Miscanthus sinensis »Zebrinus«
Nothofagus antarctica
Oenothera missouriensis
Oenothera tetragone »Hohes Licht«
Parthenocissus tricuspidata »Veit-
    chii«
Philadelphus coronarius »Aureus«
Philadelphus x lemoinei
Potentilla fruticosa »Månelys«
Potentilla fruticosa »Tangerine«
Prunus lauracerasus »Otto Luy-
    ken«
Prunus lauracerasus »Shipkaensis«
Prunus sargentii x subhirtella
    «Accolade«
Prunus serrula
Prunus serrulata
Prunus serrulata »Kanzan«
Prunus subhirtella »Autumnalis«
Pyracantha coccinea
Pyrus salicifolia
Quercus pedunculata »Fastigiata«
Quercus palustris
Rosa »Bassino«
Rosa »Mactru Trumpeter«
Rosa moyesii
Rosa moyesii »Nevada«
Rosa »Nina Weibull«
Rosa »Parkjuweel«, colour 12 A4
Rosa »Pink Bells«
Rosa »Red Bells«

Rosa »Regensburg«
Rosa »White Bells«
Rudbeckia ful. var. speciosa
Salix alba »Liempde«
Salvia nemorosa
Sedum spectabile »Carmen«
Skimmia japonica
Sorbus intermedia
Sorbus serotina
Sorbus thuringiaca »Fastigiata«
Spiraea x arguta
Spiraea x bumalda »Anthony
    Waterer«
Spiraea x vanhouttii Syringa CV
Stephanandra incisa »Crispa«
Stranvaesia davidiana
Symphoricarpus chenaultii
    »Hancock«
Taxus baccata
Taxus baccata »Adpressa Aurea«
Taxus baccata »Fastigiata«
Taxus baccata »Fastgiata Aureom
    arginata«
Taxus baccata »Dovastoniana
    Pendula«
Taxus baccata, hedge
Taxus baccata »Overeynderi«
Taxus baccata »Repandens«
Taxus baccata »Semperaurea«
Taxus baccata »Summergold«
Taxus ssp.
Taxus x media »Hicksii«
Veronica aus. »True Blue«
Veronica officinalis
Viburnum burkwoodii
Viburnum plicatum
Vinca major
Vinca minor
Weigela florida »Variegata«
    »Zwergschneeflocke«